A SIMMERING

NORMAN HADLEY

Copyright © 2018 Norman Hadley

All rights reserved.

ISBN: **978-1717069412**

FOREWORD

The excuse, "a woman made me do it" may have been around since Adam was caught scrumping an Egremont Russet, but this snake here will back me up. In the New Year of 2013/14, a poet called Jo Bell made a resolution. In an act of surpassing generosity, she undertook to create a poetry community and feed it with a new poetry prompt every week for a year. The prompts wouldn't just be some shallow "write about your cat" hokum but would be stuffed full of imaginative tinder, including poems by the Great and Good. Thus was born, "52".

In an ill-advised moment waiting for a flight, I signed up. The experience was electrifying – having Jo set up a residency inside my head for a whole year was a kind of benign possession that no exorcist would dare tamper with. Meanwhile, she had also invaded the every waking thought of around five hundred poets around the world, all responding to the prompts and all responding to each other's responses. Electricity was magnified to the pitch of a lightning storm.

This book is a selection from the five hundred and fifty poems that I wrote during that tumultuous year. I could have assembled them all, as a warts-and-all diary, but some of them were very warty indeed. Conversely, I could have culled them down to the size of a "normal" poetry collection. But I wanted to gather a broader sample of my output because the breadth itself acquired its own purpose – forcing me to mine topics and inhabit voices outside my usual range. Which leads me on to this:

Poetry isn't autobiography. Nobody arrested Johnny Cash for shooting a man in Reno just to watch him die. Poets, though, often labour under the assumption that all first-person material is literally true. Some of it is, some of it isn't. But, you get the picture, it's all the Truth.

To maintain fidelity with the genesis of the poems, I've preserved the week number. I'd heartily recommend Jo's book of prompts called, pithily, "52" as well as the anthology from the group, "The Very Best of 52". Both are published by Nine Arches Press, as is Jo's dazzling second collection, "Kith" and her informative guide, "How to Be a Poet", co-written with Nine Arches director Jane Commane.

ACKNOWLEDGMENTS

There isn't enough kudos in the world to scatter upon the head of Jo Bell for setting up 52 . But I'm also grateful to the many members of the group who took time to make thoughtful and constructive responses to these pieces. In particular, with all the associated risk of missing someone out:

Ailsa Holland
Ben Banyard
Bernie Cullen
Beth McDonough
Carole Bromley
Catherine Ayres
Cathy Dreyer
Charlotte Ansell
The late Clive Dee
Dru Marland
Elizabeth Williamson
Emma Simon
Gram Joel Davies
Hannah Linden
Hilary Robinson
Jane Burn
Jinny Fisher
Joanne Key
John Lanyon
The late John Mackie
John Mills
The late Judith Williamson
Julian Dobson
Julie Gardner
Kathy Gee
Kevin Reid
Kymm Coveney
Lesley Quayle
Lesley Reid
Liz Mills
Mandy McDonald
Maggie McKay
Marilyn Francis
Marilyn Hammick
Mary Norton Gilonne
Myfanwy Fox

Natalie Shaw
Nicky Phillips
Nikki Magennis
Nina Lewis
Nina Simon
Peter Kerr
Rachael Clyne
Rachel McGladdery
Rayya Ghul
Rebecca Gethin
Roz Goddard
Sally Evans
Sarah Bryson
Sarah L Dixon
Sarah Watkinson
Scott Edward Anderson
Seth Crook
Sharon Larkin
Simon Williams
Sophia Blackwell
Stella Wulf
Sue Kindon
Sue Millard
Susan Castillo Street
Susan Taylor
Tom Sastry
Zelda Chappell

Beyond all that, there will always be boundless gratitude to Life-Companion-Of-My-Choosing, Deb Hadley. Just because.

52.2 Traveller

I am old - the calendar insists on this.

Slippering around my carpeted domain,

between the pantry and the couch,

I want for nothing or, to be precise, no thing.

From time to time, I pull the heavy curtain back,

scan down the dusty lane that brought me

and when a sandalled pilgrim comes,

bearing on their back the dipping sun,

I squeeze a chalice brimmed with bramble juice

and press it to their lips which,

if they know the script, they will not part in speech

but go, perhaps the subtlest nod will say what's needed then

as I did when I came this way

and took the old man's trembling gift.

52.4 Proposal

I cannot offer, will not offer

rich delights for sybarites,

no scatter-cushioned, languid nest,

no chocolates in easy reach, no cheeky red.

I cannot offer, will not offer, mortgaged futures,

shares in extra-virgin North Sea oil,

no car that automatically drives

us to an index-linked demise.

I cannot offer, will not offer

coddling to fatten you

for well-intentioned slaughter

on dependency's unholy altar.

Instead, I offer you a moon

as high and wide as a fairground ride,

our crampon claws velocirapting Lochnagar,

breath-freeze hissing, shooting stars.

A SIMMERING

I offer you a dance on dawn-lit pinnacles,

ropelines maypoling the Chamonix Aiguilles,

spinneretting down to granulated glaciers,

teetering on snow-bridges of Damocles.

I offer you a bothy on a Knoydart beach,

shingle-sitting by the story-telling embers,

tongue-tips tingling with Talisker

and one another.

I offer you a hand, its knuckles granite-calloused

but slide a ring beyond these bruises - it will stay

till all the Alps have crumpled into Africa

and Lochnagar is ground away.

52.5 A Walk in Dog-Eat-Dog Wood

In a smoke-filled snug, somewhere beyond our sight

Badger is explaining

he's a better badger (simple, really)

than the one what didn't see the lights.

Sparrowhawk's opining that it's evolution, innit?

Stands to reason if you 'aven't got the turn of speed,

yer prolly better

as a pile of scattered feathers.

Gangsta-Cuckoo, leaning on the bar,

is holding court on where the Meadow Pipit

made her great mistake.

Too bad the nest was on display to Ma.

Take no comfort from our deepwood saunterings, my child,

as we go tiptoeing past screaming Stoat and mewling Shrew.

All animals are insufferable right-wingers

and the converse is equally true.

52.5 Logpile Butterfly

In winter, it is always time to fetch the firewood in.

The stove's a hungry Oliver

that twists my lumber into braids of flame.

Today, the morning sun

has newly crept round to the shed.

I lift a layer of steaming logs to see

a Peacock, winter-hunkered,

folded in the darkness of itself.

Unfurling wings, it flashes me a voodoo glare

but I'm not scared, until

it rasps - the drythroat irritation

of the prematurely woken.

Tell me, Schmetterling, is this breaking fast too soon for you?

I proffer summer honeys on a jam jar lid,

kindling this smoulder of spring

in cupped palms.

52.5 Windwolf

The only howl I've heard so far

is bounceback from the walls of Buachaille Etive Beag

so I lope on, through belly-depths of heather,

bucking scuts of snow, a spatchcocked hare.

Two nights ago, a man, his glinting blade,

released me from my concrete-padded cell.

From deep within his greying muzzle

called me "Stone of Destiny" and gave me song.

I dash myself on night-flight impulses

from Achtriochtan banks to Rannoch Moor,

a stranger to exhaustion, lollop-tongued,

a fangclamp on the windpipe of the world.

A squirm of new beginnings in my sag

I sniff the wind for signals, slink to fank.

52.6 All Day in Bed

Dog-tongue-hot, and not a hope we'd stick a toe

beyond the moat of our newlywed bed.

Hand-me-down nets billowed open windows,

gutters creaked an inexpensive song

under burdens of sparrows and infra-red.

In the street, a giggle of children busied fingers

in a game they probably don't play anymore.

And we to ours, never out of fashion,

wallowing our toast-crumb nest,

pillow-bolstered against ordinary opinions,

swimming coloured pages of liberal supplements,

chin-dripping fruits for breakfast and sex on the hour.

The sun slunk, reluctant,

a helium balloon too taut on its tethering.

I only got up to pull the window shut

when the spindrift started blowing in.

52.6 Stürmische Nacht

The blindfold sky is throwing knives.

We're handcuffed to a spinning board,

our audience, this Wagner-ring of peaks,

a wall-of-death for echo-roars.

The dark's a canvas, jagged by daggerlight.

We clench all night to the tip of our steeple,

ladderless jacks, weather-cocky, squeaking

as we swing, hunch-backed, inside the clangour.

We tie crude crucifixes from our axes,

mutter less-than-Christian invocations,

hedging bets with Thor and Zeus, our metal fizzing sparks,

the searchlight finds you and your hair's a pencil-gonk of charge.

Your head tilts back in laughter and a Yorick grin

emerges from your skin in negative.

The polaroid that's flapping in my hand depicts

an x-ray of a fatalist.

52.7 Gymnast

Lissom as her ribbon,

she patters birdprints and

briefly becomes air.

52.8 The Volvo Suicides

The town is twinned with Anhedonia.

The kids keep tallies on their wrists.

Each day they've lolled, a pallid denim

tidewash on the council office steps,

gawping at the upright bronzes, Gloriously Dead.

When blades get blunted by experience,

they hose their fathers' cars with Hoover tubing,

squeezing five abreast, ingesting gases diaphragm-deep.

But Sweden's engineers have thought of this,

the bong innocuously catalysed, they crack the door,

to slither home for Strictly and a plate that once was warm.

They'll keep on trying to transcend their parish boundaries,

squealing wheels around the bypass,

moth-sick for the brightest lamppost.

When the radiator steam has blown away,

they're still airbagged, safety-caged.

52.8 Stray

This old cat has straggled far beyond

the twittens of his kittenhood.

He's whiskered twitchells, dozed in chares,

slunk, belly-level, down jennels and vennels,

keened for yowling queens in weinds

and pined for scraps in wynds.

He's faced down spitting bullies

in littered gullies, arched his back

at bigger cats, loitering

the jiggers by the council flats,

been cornered in shuts, snuck

through snickelways, sloped down opes.

The cities he has flickered through remain

a labyrinth to him, brick walls soaring, closing in.

52.8 About Our Street

Mama says our street has changed; she says

the windows where the ladies sit

were filled with flowers.

Mama says the building

where the ladies do the dancing

used to gleam with curtain poles.

Mama drops me at the minder's,

picks me up with lipstick everywhere.

52.9 How We Settle Things Now

The poet, wearying of bullies, publically challenged

Vlad the Invader to combat, mano-a-mano.

Interpreters on flashing hotlines nodded frowns,

"He lose, he give the other country back."

Vlad strode the arena, bare-chested though the night was freezing,

dead grass drooping from his plastic antlers.

The poet showed up, resplendent in a sequinned jockstrap

accessorised with a lamé cape which he frisbeed off,

cleared his throat and spoke,

"Pawn to king four."

52.9 World Peace

(or How we settle things now, 2)

When women took control of world affairs,

the missile silos filled with cobwebs,

warheads broken down for parts.

The only sound the clink of spoons

as mothers took their daughters out to tea

and little ploshes as they dropped

in one another's cup the tiny cubes of plutonium.

52.9 Revelation

It was on a sullen Tuesday

the email arrived, addressed

to all.users@universe.the

admitting that the brain-in-vat-hypothesis

was absolutely true and nobody existed,

not in any sense that mattered.

Everyone cheered (or would have, given lungs)

to think that Hitler didn't really kill

a single person and they didn't have

to go to work on Wednesday and

no need to really die as long as

no-one nudged the power off.

By Friday, all the network cables thrummed

with one electric thought:

"How lonely are you, now?"

52.9 Born Again

The medics had perfected the electrodes,

the audience voted for a child-to-be to be the first.

They wired his forehead up in utero and plugged him in.

Extruded down the birth canal, his senses flooded out

in ones and zeroes.

In shower-caps of wires around the world,

a billion suppressed memories gasped into the light.

52.9 Life Story

born

boon

loon

lion

lien

lies

dies

52.9 "It Was An Accident..."

Mum and Dad bought Him

a chemistry set. A Bang.

"Big? Compared to what?"

52.9 White rabbits. White rabbits. White rabbits.

No use drumming tearful fists against the chest of this:

You're tearing off the perforated edges of another month;

a thousand such, your skull's a wormery or windblown dust.

So poke your head out from the speeding car:

your gasp is snagging in your throat. At first,

you purse your lips as though around a final smoke.

Now, seize control of your jolted breathing.

Con

cen

trate

and

grin

into the windrush.

52.9 A New Beginning

When the Wilsons judged

that they were halfway through the marriage,

they hired a jobbing surgeon-friend

to sever their heads

to sew back on

but swapped around.

They spent their second twenty years

apologising for a million insensitivities

but the sex was fantastic.

52.9 Magic Eye Book

My mother tricked me into poetry.

Dying, Emily Dickinson on her bedside table,

and a fly in the room I didn't notice at the time.

I was Science, entrapped in a web of graphs.

Instead of lines, she handed me a book of clever dots,

computed to confuse the eye, I had to hold it right,

unhinge the gimbals of my focus till the dots would shoal

and coalesce, a dolphin wheeling through my head,

squealing laughter at a literalist condemned

forever to stare through the page.

52.10 Breakfast of Champions

Crunchy toast,

wobbly eggs,

crispy fritters,

oozy jam,

freshly-squeezed

wife.

52.10 Unputdownable

All the poetry,

from Hafez to Donne,

anthologised

in the sleek Braille

of your body.

52.10 Call to the Centre

Thank you for calling Hathaway, Ellis and Lumsden Ltd.

To speak to one of our trained operators, please press 6.

All calls are monitored for...purposes.

Please type your 36-digit personal account number followed by the hash key.

In case of error, simply redial.

Please press 6

Please list sins in alphabetical order, grouping repeat offences.

For example, "shoplifting, three times"

Remember to enunciate clearly.

In case of error, simply redial.

Please press 6.

Your afterlife *is* important to us.

52.10 Abseil

A slick umbilical to something solid

so he lowers, hand over trembling hand

and, every thousand feet or so,

the texture changes. Here, it's hawser-laid

in brightly coloured nylon; lower down,

a hairy twist of sisal strands.

Speed increases,

clinging tighter only burns the palms.

Somewhere down beneath the torch's reach,

an end. He often thinks of this,

the fraying fibres running through his fingers,

a last caress of Lizzie Siddal's hair.

52.11 The Hills My Father Gave Me

From shattered ridges
where you no longer go,
I bring you flakes of quartz.

From frosted summit cairns,
where you once hunkered
from the howling,

I bring photographs:
those rectangles of light
and lies that telescope

a ten-mile sweep
of mountainside
to six by four.

Mostly, I bring poems; you
can tuck them in your pillow where
their rustling will keep you wakeful.

Down-swaddled in your lowland bed,
your tread will rise and float
on hills as old as solemn youth
where you go
following me,
following you.

52.11 Hymn to the Gàidhlig

My English lips are murmuring a prayer
in a tongue my mother didn't know,
the cantering flow of Sgurr Leac nan Each,
the jagged kerf of Stuc a Choire Duibhe Bhic.

I hope to win A'Mhaighdean, drape her
with the jewels of Beinn Alligin.
I'll forge my vowels in An Teallach's fire,
lick the hiss where Sula Bheinn anvils the sky.

My finger feels the lethal tang of compass needles,
my eyes the blades of Cuillin slicing Coir Uisg spume,
still my palate undulates, feminine as a heather swell,
with the dappled lilt of Sgurr Cos na Breachd-laoidh.

Sgurr = 'skoor' = peak. Stuc is also a peak.
Leac = 'lekk' - rock
na and nan = of the
Choire = 'horry' = corrie
Duibhe = "dooey" = black
Bhic = 'veek' = small
Mhaighdean = 'vay-chun' = maiden
Beinn = hill. Pronunciation can vary from Ben to Byne
Alligin = jewel
An Teallach = 'chellak' = the forge
Cos = cave . The s is a bit like that in 'measure'
Breachd - 'Brecht' = dappled
Laoidh - 'Loo-ee' = calf

52.11 Syllabus

To get an education, study mathematics.
Snip the guy ropes from your fat balloon
and float into the blue; caress
the smooth austerity of π r squared and four-thirds π r cubed.

When you have danced patterns round the Argand Diagram
and slipped your sledge's runners down a million equals signs,
then study physics. Span your compasses across the forces
driving planets, apples, atoms; let your prisms splinter light.

When you've spun the fundamental particles between your digits,
lift your vision from the nucleus, to swim among electron-clouds.
Count charge and countercharge, the yin and yang of valency,
feasting at the banquet-symmetry of Mendeleev's table.

With mastery of Chemistry, hammer rocks, slake lime from stone,
smelt lustrous sheets of bronze from malachite, then
creak your atlas open, push pins where early cities sprang
as copper trickles from the fertile earth, trace histories

of peoples nourished by glow of gold and grain,

then track their words, their cultures and philosophies

across the jigsawn continents.

Having grappled language and the clean, Aegean light of logic,

then, and only then, go back

and study mathematics.

52.12 Meteor Shower

Beyond the usual indifference,

the universe threw rocks at us.

The sky stretched out a hand

and snatched up every one

with light-trails safely singeing

through our upturned vision, as if

we were mittened children,

not yet trusted with sparklers.

52.12 Sky-Father

Lying on their backs,

the Proto-Indo-Europeans

squinted at the *dyeu* so blue,

to catch a glimmer of their *pihter*.

Apollo slung their grandsons out

beyond the moon, to see if *Dyeu-Pihter*

was hidden there but, looking back, they saw,

for all that time, they'd been lying on his eye.

52.13 Learning Fish

You can give a child the word 'fish.'
It will lie, pouting and bug-eyed
on the picture-book slab.

Three days later,
whiffing on the midden of the mind,
then a cartoon ladder of bones.

Or

stroke its rainbow brilliancy together,
swish its tail through crystal scales of
watery Geordie song.

Bob floats on the night-lit ripples of the f.
Slide blades along the spine of the i.
Get Sean Connery to kish the fricative.

Hook a line to history, to tax in Latin baskets,
scribe ichthys eyes on the fisher of men,
draw in the net, separate the good from bad.

Then stop; as,
topped and tailed,
fish just is.

52.13 Happiness

I have held water,

trickling through

ring-gapped fingers.

I have held hot coal,

my fingers seared with ancient

trees re-entering the atmosphere

I have held a nuthatch

not too tightly,

like the lady showed me.

I opened my palm; the bird

quivered, blinked at freedom,

took wing.

52.13 Love Lines

Just as the French have mapped the Arrondissements of kisses,

there are lines all over England - swooping, cursive isoglosses,

showing where the women call you 'love'.

They ladle it like custard over sponge;

it gloops down through your ear.

The heat and waist-expanding slurp of it will swaddle

in your belly, give you strength to last till tea.

Be wary where they say it 'lav,' as if

the throne for some Great Bowel Shift.

No. Listen to it treacle down Guy Garvey's larynx

or spread the clotted burr of 'loverrr' over scones

and, setting root, pore over maps

for where the warm fronts lie.

52.13 Sand

It takes another roughness

to make a rough thing smooth;

ask any carpenter's son.

It takes a softness

to vanquish Saharasia,

drowning Kings of Kings.

Even as the imprints

of our fleeting castles

are rinsed by tideswish,

it is hissing through

the corset-waist

of its own clear self.

Blake's worlds,

swirling from dunes,

smarting our eyes.

52.13 Eating the Noggin

Yes, I was that satchel-
swinging, untucked shirt,
Laurie-Leeing to her kitchen
every afternoon.

The bread was always just
from the oven, overflowing,
needing trimming,
butter dripping.

Yes, I was that boy
and that is why
you should not marry me
and why you should.

52.13 In the Coppice of Ideas

Come, pass the billhook, hold the saw and look
among the hazel withies - this is where
Montaigne came reaping; later, Hughes and Plath
came arm-in-arm with bundled rushes held

by plashed and brash-strewn banks. Find knotted cuts
where Milton swung his blade to trim the frost-
rimed stems that Shakespeare left as residue,
who gathered Chaucer's leavings in the rain.

Keep wandering in woods where Plato walked
behind the hemlock-bitter blade of Socrates.
But cut with care; it will spring back to span
repeating centuries of ancient thought.

   There's plenty more will follow after you
   so only help yourself to what you're due.

52.13 Daylight Saving Time

I tried to buy an hour once, the woman took the money
and was gone; the hour followed in her train,
as desiccated flowers on a dusty, bridal hem
towards a clock tower whose four faces disagreed.

I tried alighting from the train a while, to find a halt
that Beeching never heard of, creak into a settle
thick with cat-fur, rail-rust swallowed up in Buddleia
and listen to the kettling of a distant whistle.

These minutes may be unforgiving, malice-fanged
or vast as star-gaps, hour by hour
the fluid drizzles through the muslin, cleansed
of meaning, try to snatch it and it will not catch your eye.

My finger crooks the minute-hand. I'll only claw this hour back
by kicking through the torn-up promises of summer.

52.14 Unladen

To shrug a heavy rucksack from your shoulders

is a drug - the lightness craved by those admitted

into eating clinics: to be excused from Newton's rules

and leap a lunar crater wider than the waiting room

where we once heard those whispered words,

"All clear".

52.14 Gingerbread Cutter

The gingerbread cutter in my drawer

is a man with a boy-shape hollowed out.

Hold him up to the window's glare;

there's nothing there. A squeeze

between your finger and your thumb

and he collapses, but he bounces back

and doesn't rust.

52.14 Postholes

An archaeologist once told me that
a hole outlasts most relics of the past.
The subtle shifts of colour in the soil betray
where spades have cut through earth and worms.

I knew a man. He taught me how to dig
a hole through gloopy clay. He showed the way
to set the fencepost straight, to tap it back
and forth until the bubble hit its mark.

I sometimes go down to his woods – amidst
the flop of bluebells, fences that we made
still keep the beasts at bay. A hole remains.
An absence joined by others every day.
The Portland cliffs could slough away a tonne
of Postcrete; still, it wouldn't be enough.

52.14 Unfound

A flapping leg beneath the summit

so I summoned help.

A dozen bobbing torches

slit the drizzle

so I blew my whistle.

I shouted names of all the saints

but they just looked right through me

and stretchered away the silence.

52.14 Really Gone

An absence of an absence

is another absence

as I found, the fortieth night.

Dousing the light and clicking through

the abacus of the day, it seemed

I hadn't thought of you at all.

Staring at my eyelids,

I willed the blackness back.

52.15 Triplex Toughened

A raked pane shoulders the gale,

as stoic as the insects that it blatts

from air to smear.

A world of wind-blown dust outside;

in here, it's cool as a catacomb, except

that image in the glass:

before the world of clunk and click,

the pillowy receiving of the airbag,

Alice in the left-hand seat,

a skim of frost, the steering light;

she flew to meet her own reflection,

passing through it.

My fingers stretch out to the screen,

that fragile membrane

separating her from me.

52.15 Bell, Book and Candle

The bell muffles the wind that comes fluting

through a stone tower. The Father listens

to its founded tonnes holding silence down,

hung above a congregation of one.

The book is the trees, rustling their truth

from an afterlife we can never chart:

first came the word and the word was written

on trees felled by an axe, wielded by the wordless.

The candle summons sacraments of light

from the tallow of a butchered lamb;

both weep their whole selves over slabs of oak,

dissolving artefact to crimson stain.

Everywhere the Father looks, things are

exorcising themselves of their own nature.

52.15 A History of Violence

The grains in the blade

remember every blow

of the Sheffield hammer,

the grip of rusted tongs

over hissing coals.

The handle remembers

the saw that unskeletonned

a bleating creature, now

flopping useless in the corner

of the abattoir.

The knife sits on the table,

twitches in the fluctuations

of magnetic fields and

hungers for your belly.

52.16 Seventy Years Old

When the gods breathed into him, "threescore years
and ten shalt thou labour and sorrow," he noticed
they hadn't said consecutive.

So he lived a year, saw Ur rise, died for ninety-nine
then lived again. Each time, waking from a century dead,
the world had borne itself to somewhere new.

In childhood, he witnessed the dribble of bronze
from smelted rocks; as a man, the whiter heat of iron.
In later years, he heard a furnace hiss with steam.

I remember him, eyes swirling with seven millennia.
He handed me a book, was cut off and flew away.

52.16 Category Errors

Miss Nesbitt tapped the blackboard.

"What's the square root of disappointment?
Or the reciprocal of Tuesday?
Who's the Prime Minister of forty seven?
And what's the capital of twenty three?

A mathematician writing poems
is a tourist, lost in Oxford,
asking directions
for the University."

I wrote a Euclid proof on one side of a strip
of paper, Sonnet Eighteen ("see, they're numbered")
on the other. A twist of wrist, a dab of tape,
I made a ring of Mobius.

I took her hand, ran her lacquered nails
around the surface and replied,

"The result of all our learning

is returning where we started

but inverted. There's no making

sense of knots in time or trying

to trick the clock by looping twice

to find yourself the right way up.

The knotsmith's thought of that."

52.16 Marked

Sixth child of six.

Born at number six at 6am.

Letters in his first and last

name - you can do the maths.

Six years old, he's shaving

his head, looking for signs.

52.16 Round Riddle

Yes. I love a maths conundrum,

to circle round its blank

diameter, measuring.

Mystery parameter,

god of the circular area,

seduce my senses

with the raw, majestic hum

of numbers recurring never...

52.16. Laiku

Westerners aping

oriental syllables

isn't really *on*.

52.16 Splitting the Difference

So much bloodshed

arguing one God or three

by people made from two.

52.16 House Numbers

The measure of a household

isn't headcount but the number

of relationships: the chinks of glass

when Dad gets speechy.

There were twenty-eight at home until

my brother flew then, with the fleeing sisters,

twenty-one, then fifteen, ten and six.

I was last to leap from the eaves; that final meal,

three clinks of glass. Then, just the one.

52.17 Dippers

The heat had come to Cumbria.

The Old Man of Coniston

wanted for a knotted hanky.

We slunk down to the Duddon,

splashing its sonnets over boulders,

the dripping sleekness of her.

That skirtless curtsey, that song:

the tinkling pitch of cinclus-cinclus

cutting through running waters.

52.17 Bluetit Broods

Shaving the lawn to a baize this morning,

I heard the thin, insistent tseep of Bluetit

babies gaping for an aphid-laden beak.

This pleasure's tinged, as pleasures are.

Was it only a month ago, I angled my ladder

to the birch to clean the nest-box out?

I'd found that last year's brood had not succeeded;

scattered in that casket: seven sets of hair's-breadth bones

written out of history, like princes in a tower.

52.17 Acting on Impulse

I don't know why. Just yesterday,
we hunkered in the treetops
waiting for the sleet to clear.

Today, I don't know why,
I want to scream my head off
at the milk float trundling by.

Something dimly tells me
there is something in this
T-junction I must control.

I also want to pick up sticks.
I cannot help it. Something's
making me arrange them in a disc.

I faintly recollect a bowl like this,
another bird arriving, bearing worms.
Is that what this is leading to?

The other day, I caught myself
striking lamp-post poses,
bowing to no-one. I don't know why.

Suddenly, I've got this urge
to stand on your back and
rub our bums together.

So all I can do is stand on this branch
and scream and scream,
"I don't know why! I don't know why!"

52.17 Bittern

Deep in the rustling reeds, I listened
for that bottle-blowing boom.

Every morning, in my diligence,
I jotted down the latitude and longitude,
triangulating echoes in the feathered
muffling overtopping me.

Plotting on the map, I saw,
around the Wash, the Humber
Estuary and Dungeness,
a line of foghorns
strung along the Saxon shore.

52.17 Curlew

Even now, I hear that song,

I smell Cumbrian earth

punctured by a tent-peg.

Creaking from the car to set up camp,

that lonesome fluting overhead. We were,

in every sense that mattered, home.

52.17 A Mute Swan

He kept her indoors, her skin

as pale as a wedding gown.

He liked her slim as when he

found her. Liked to do the talking.

When he was out in the world,

she'd sometimes kneel

to kiss her own reflection

in the glassy table top,

for human contact.

When he didn't return,

she padded carpets seven days,

then swelling airs uncrinkled her lungs,

unleashing Puccini.

The table shattered.

52.17 A Charm of Goldfinches

Tilting the bike down a stitchwort-fringed lane,

the outriders appear from blackthorn hedges

flitting round my wheel, their singing trickles

liquid metal on their wings like finger-bells in flight.

52.17 For a Linnet

She had a fondness for hemp;

her floaty-skirted smallness

wouldn't fit in any cage.

The bangles on her wrists

recounted former captors

and her trilling in the night

still turns me to a blush.

52.17 Lyall's Wren

The Island was shouty with wrens.

No one ate them which was bonza

so they didn't bother flying any more.

Then Captain Cook got bored

with Yorkshire, because

they were rubbish at cricket.

So he sailed the ocean blue

(or was that someone else?)

introducing need to empty seas.

Ships needed a lighthouse, needing

a keeper, needing company, setting

the cat basket down like a Gary Larson cartoon.

Tibbles (I kid you not)

patrolled the cliffs

and licked the silence clean.

52.18 Naming It

A man called Ransome

showed me how it's not enough

to teeter out to the furthest rock

in the rush of river, that you had

to name it, had

to own it,

so when you crouched

where the wagtails pirouetted

and the river splashed your sandals

you would, making sure that

no one else could hear you, whisper,

'Finisterre,

Finisterre.'

52.18 Cumbria's Santiago

All Lakeland hiking is a pilgrimage,

so flatten the map and find your destination.

Yes, you could head for the rich effulgence

of Buttermere, the languid meanders of Patterdale.

But you're English, of the House of Windsor (Babs),

your knees are bent to Sid James of Compostela,

your heritage is pinging bras on campsites,

flicking vees at Frenchy's phalanx.

So, the route's decided and the

band of journeyers proceeds

on all (muddy) fours

to Breasty Haw.

52.19 Co-education

We chewed our pencil ends together over nine times tables or
Red-Rovered hopscotched playgrounds hand-in-hand, until that
afternoon the nurse led all the girls away in scenes of sepia
like something from The World At War.

We boys scuffed shoes beneath our ink-welled desks, to guess
at what was going on beyond the wall. A few had elder sisters;
there were days on sofas, sea-shelled round hot-water bottles,
cursing something we should not expect to comprehend.

I asked Miss Thompson why we weren't invited; she insisted
this was not our business - what use could we be? I wasn't sure
but thought of fetching wobbly cups of tea, of patting hair
and nodding that it wasn't fair.

Language shifted; everything was whispers, sometimes snippets
leaked through fingers but you had to tear through seven layers
of bubble wrap, unpack the euphemisms carefully constructed
to conceal all meaning in their ambiguity.

A SIMMERING

So Jenn was 'on' as if she had a lightbulb somewhere underneath
her uniform. Or Katie's mum had reached a 'certain' age
but nothing seemed less certain. Questions soaked my mind
just like a you-know-what, of how it felt to find a woman's shape
erupting through your ribcage, or that conjuring trick
that formed a pelvic cradle from your swelling hips.

When longing looking turned to touch, I asked you should I press
a little firmer, slower, higher up? Backed by your team
of *Just Seventeen* advisors, you knew it wasn't ladylike to say.
I was supposed to know. So when you rolled your eyes
at my incompetence and told your friends I didn't understand,
I didn't.

52.19 Learning the Truth About Kingfishers

The planet lost a little of its patina

the day he told me that a kingfisher's

not really blue. "Oh no," he intoned,

"there's not a hint of pigment

in their plumage. Deep in shade,

they fade to just another LBJ."

It seems that something in their feather-hairs

can scatter sun to conjure colour from a blur of air,

as if there is a world of brilliance somewhere

the bird reveals as it unzips the river.

(LBJ= 'little brown job' in birders' parlance)

52.19 On First Seeing Keats in Ransome

I was in thrall to his ability

to fashion Kangchenjunga

from a Lakeland fell.

Only later did I see

that Titty's speech

on Darien was Keats.

And later still that Keats

was praising Chapman,

channeller of Homer:

a human chain to link

me to antiquity, to vow

that if I had a daughter

I would take her sailing

on Aegean Coniston

and pass it on.

52.19 Not Worthy

The gods, as usual, amused themselves.

"Let's give him strength," they said,

"he cannot use," then went to town

on her with every natural advantage:

assets soon enhanced by Top Shop,

Rimmel and La Senza. Then Anita Roddick

lathered her with unguents condensed

from some Angolan berry he'd not heard of.

So this penitent is down on carpet-dimpled knees

at this asymmetry, the only sound his broken throat

can make is 'please' and she's as patient as a simile

that's better left unsaid as all-he-has-to-offer's wept

into her emptiness.

52.19 Boys (and Girls) Are Rubbish

There was a spat. The spark was not

recorded. Rival lines appeared across

the playground, jeering slogans

later disavowed in sweaty discotheques

but, just for now, a lonely figure stands

in no-man's-land, a football in his

Christmas hand, his Pie Jésu voice

is trebling, "Both are brilliant!" and still

he's wondering when armistice begins.

52.20 To Abraham

Tell me how the blade felt

dimpling his throat.

Tell me the relief of letting go.

Tell me how many other sons

would later lie, bayoneted

by obedience.

Tell me of the chance you had

to bellow back, at that command,

"Go kill your own!"

52.20 Love Letter to Mary Wollstonecraft

How we've let you down, your heirs in thought; it seems we've

barely started or are heading back. Two centuries have passed

since "Vindication" catapulted from the printing press and one

since Charlotte Perkins Gilmour pointed at a Lady's Hat,

it's still a matter of debate if heels empower or belittle,

whether cloth across the face degrades or liberates.

I looked for easy answers with my mechanistic mind, soon bound

in paradox. I hold your intellect in such respect, yet yearn to hold

you small and, yes, to press you to the bed. I'm full of paradox

myself. I want to sweep down from the sky on glowing wings

to pull you back from the crumbling river parapet. I want

to warn you irony's at hand, you are with child again

and this will be your end; as bright a light as Mill's or Paine's

put out by something so mammalian.

52.21 The Dream-Curse of Gregor Samsa

Do not go to sleep tonight,

or I will summon pressure

in your abdomen and split

the skin to either side; new

legs will sprout below your

thorax and the ones you had

will tingle as the hairs grow

thick and rigid as your

forehead germinates,

antennae stretch towards

the headboard; stay awake,

avoid this fate; keep your

eyes wide open, staring

into compound darknesses.

52.21 Interceptions

Here's a poem all about a dragonfly;
there's shimmering, of course,
and iridescence.

Remember, though, that poem
all about a speeding windscreen?

Here's a poem all about a Monarch
Butterfly and there'll be fluttering
aplenty through the stratosphere.

But let me just remind you: we were
talking of the appetite of turbofans.

Everywhere, the beautiful and delicate
collides with rigid circumstance
and, by an act of will, we also
call this beautiful.

52.21 Brimstone

The devil rises from the earth in March,

scribbles his signature in air

with a highlighter pen the colour

of the last retch.

52.21 Emerald Cockroach Wasp

The dance begins with a sting.

She tarantella-steps around him,

jabs again, the venom sinking in.

He staggers backwards, slumps

to knees, she reaches up, her mouth-parts

slowly chewing through his semaphore-antennae so

he can not signal shame at being led away, the stone

rolled into place, the larva knowing

which internal organs to consume and

in which order so his flesh stays fresh

for long enough to liberate another wasp

to fly up to its loving God.

52.21 Aphids - A Tabloid Week

GREENFACED INVADERS TARGET UK GARDENS

IMMIGRANT POPULATION SOARS 300% IN A WEEK

FATHERS WHO NEVER KNEW THEIR YOUNG

THE SINGLE MOTHERS SUCKING BRITAIN DRY

BORN PREGNANT - THE SHOCKING TRUTH

LADYBIRD STRIKE FEARS - LATEST

NO ENGLISH ROSE SAFE

52.21 From the Strong

boy-cook

syrup tin

bee riddle

lion roar

Samson sinew

skin split

larvae feast

honey-comb

boy nod

cake oven

mother death

larvae feast

boy wisdom

boy strength

man sweetness

52.22 Parley

We might be born between the shit and piss;

we'll maybe end our days in brittlebony ravings;

just for now, let's crystallise this instant,

Dali-melt our watches in our fire and gallop

through the sparkblown dark with bleeding spurs

pressed deep in stallion-sides and laughing low

at hanging branches, vaulting fences neither horse

nor rider sees, your hair a tangle of perfection

and your thunder-pulse in synchrony

with drumming hooves so when we fetch up,

lathered, by a stream the beasts lap dry,

we'll light another fire and lie in the wild-moon roaring of it.

52.22 Adventures in Imaginary Numbers

After a few months' studying imaginary numbers, we spotted the tautology: all numbers are imaginary, for how could you ever have two apples when apples are not identical? You can have an apple and a slightly different apple so two is imaginary, too. We wandered around the Argand Diagram for a while, then went back into the cave where Plato's people cowered from the shadows. We counted them out of habit, of course, but shook our heads wisely at the result. We studied light and found it was perhaps a thing or possibly a ripple in another thing. We thought of matter for a while, of how it might be here, or there or nowhere all at once and how cats both were and weren't and contented ourselves with uncertainty. We proved God's nonexistence by talking it over with Him and eventually they gave us certificates so we could get jobs and work in offices and fill in virtual forms on screens made of matter emitting light that may or may not exist to depict numbers that bear only the vaguest resemblance to reality under a watchful nonexistent eye and happiness grew at 2.9% per annum so everybody cheered.

52.23 Bobby Fischer's Game of the Century

Jeezus, who's this snotnosed brat?

And when's he gonna swell

to fill his papa's borrowed suit?

Thirteen years ya say?

Well this'll be a lion toying

with a chaffinch. This, I gotta see.

Byrne has white. He moves

his pieces like he's idling

salt and pepper down the diner.

Fischer's twitchy but it seems

he knows his way around a fianchetto.

What the heck? He's offered up a knight

but Byrne has seen right through it;

now the kid just lets the old man

take his queen, as if it's nothing to him

and the row of homburgs at the back

nods sagely, well, the kid had spirit.

What is this? He's still not finished?

Guys are coming in from other rooms

to see this; drops of sweat are racing

down Byrne's brow, and now the kid

is seeing in dimensions way beyond

the eight by eight so when Byrne's king

goes tumbling, there's silence like

Bikini Atoll when the light arrives

before the wind.

52.23 Making Wainwright's Sandwiches

Better cut 'em straight,

cos 'e'll be at 'em later

wi' 'is sodding set-square

as if Great Gable cares,

'alf-mooning down its nose

on 'im, just lolling in the grass

to scoff 'is butties, suckling 'is briar,

blowing smoke-rings of perfectionism

into Lakeland skies while I'm inside,

forever carpeted away. I dust 'is study,

where 'e pens 'is letters

to 'is many mistresses

and draws their contours

wi' an artist's lust

that never once drew me.

52.23 Seeing Churchill, Eight Weeks On

I take the news to Number Ten; the telegram's

an unexploded bomb perspiring in my hand.

Trafalgar Square, eight weeks ago: such scenes

of jubilation; Johnnies cost a penny, or a shilling new.

"Prime Minister will see you now."

He's on his second scotch. I watch him peel

the exit polls apart; he knows his Kipling

inside out, I needn't speak defeat or victory.

He gazes out across the Thames

but only sees Gallipoli.

52.23 Washing Gwen Moffat's Feet

Though eighty-nine years' old, she's steady

on the holds, her bare feet padding gabbro slabs;

there's daintiness but strength aplenty in her stance.

Reclining on the cairn of Sgurr Mhic Choinnich,

she smokes, "Too late for worrying about that now,"

still, she's barefoot, surfing down the An Stac screes;

I wince in leather boots as we shoot down to paddle

in Loch Coire Lagan where I hold each calloused foot

in cradling hands and come to understand the hardening

required to turn a nineteen-twenties' girl into a climbing guide.

52.24 My Mother's Eyes

A naming service and a funeral

within a winter's week but,

when the blue had faded,

her greenness reemerged,

looking up from my lap,

the suckling miracle of spring.

52.24 (Probably Not) My Last Word on Whether Kingfishers are Really Blue.

The breakfast bickering begins again,

as soft as feet on cathedral steps.

I talk of spectral physics; you just point

your *Quod Est Demonstrandum* finger at the bird.

I ask what colour's oil? what colour's

oil on water? which says more of oil?

So we sit, rougeing the green leaves

of essence into mere existence.

You know I'm right.

52.24 Describing Red to Helen Keller

I took her to a sunset canyon rim,

and trembled hands above a glowing coal,

felt running blood from a butchered lamb;

she signed for anger but she also drew

an image of herself, a floor-length dress,

her entering a ballroom full of men

and not one breath.

52.24 The Colour of Snow

The painter wanted to know:

what colour's snow? It takes

its context - never white,

in brightness, blue; at dusk,

an orange hearthside warmth.

I took him up a mountain

in the dark. We saw the snow

was glowing with the memory

of cloud-flight, its recent grace,

its washing down of moonlight.

52.24 Black and White

I asked the grieving father,

"just how black is that?",

imagining a coal mine

with the lamps gone flat

and no canary song.

He said, "it's just the opposite:

that torture where they sew

your eyelids back in desert sun.

There's no more night;

your optic nerves glow white

as lightbulb filaments

with all they can't unsee."

52.24 Rainbow of Containment

Primrose crib

Pink pinafore

Navy suit

White dress

Ketchup top

Lilac skirt

Black Daimler

52.25 Mountain Stream

Here, it gurgles,

bubbling under boulders; further up,

the roar of waterfalls has hacked

a cleft through mossy rocks.

The zigzags of the beck

are always tugging

at the knitting of the tarn

that never will unravel.

So I'll sit and listen to the river's song

a little longer, tip your ashes

on the tinkling waters

for that final dance downstream

to a beach I cannot see,

where squealing children

fashion castles from the

sparkling grit of your obduracy.

52.25 Man on Wire

He hears the breathing of New Yorkers far below, the whispering of winds that wouldn't move a tissue on the sidewalk. Deeper in, he hears the placid balance of the fluid in his inner ear caressing hairs to give each foot its orders on the rope: a millimetre to the left or walk - don't walk. Beyond the northern tower, in some place his focus cannot wander, comes a distant rubber squeal: an airplane greets the tarmac at La Guardia with a papal kiss.

52.25 Not Sunbathing (after Tom Sastry)

The gaffer'd taught me how to fall:

there's no use clawing at the slates

or grasping for a finial; accept it,

concentrate; arrange your limbs

and take the blow with grace.

No one heard the whumph

as I made landfall in the grass.

For passers-by, the aftermath

made perfect sense: a man

lay shirtless in the morning sun.

They hurried past to where they had to be.

I tried to call; the fall had stilled my throat.

All day, I roasted on the lawn and no one

thought it odd until the moths began

to clatter streetlamps clean.

52.26.3 Gentling

On the eighth day, tiring of rest,

He made something so beautiful

it required a special verb

for touching it.

52.27 A Catholic Mountaineer in Purgatory

I'm getting quicker now: with effort,

I could shave another twenty seconds

from the lap. My thighs could prop up

oaks and I can feel my lungs contracting

like the bellows of those fires far away.

I could recite 'Hail Mary' fifty-thousand times

but I don't yearn for fluffy clouds or harps,

the endless pleasantries or fattening

ambrosia. It's this, this death,

this endless, cleansing effort.

52.28 Six a.m.

It wouldn't matter

if the clock were hushed.

At six, my eyes pop open, wide

as my mother's bulged that day

to make each morning like a small

renaissance, flailing limbs against

constraint and clawing the hours

towards me.

52.28 The People of Eternal Dawn

Once we bought the private jet

we never fell to Earth again.

Refueling planes rose up like skylarks

bringing kerosene and bread.

We surfed the wave, just keeping pace

with the tracking of the sun:

to us, a Ferris wheel of fire

forever flaming the horizon;

incipient day our guiding light

a glow of hope, just out of sight.

52.28 Clock Hands

He's quick. In a flick of his wrist,

he can whip up a rib or a transom.

Boats rise up from the workshop floor

to the woodpecker rattle of his bone-handled chisel.

She swings her hips to the rhythm

of a spoon in jam, as languorous

as butter melting down

an angled slice of toast.

At noon, she whistles him down

his ladder; they sit amidst a scatter

of steaming bread with drips

of thyme-scent olive oil.

In the dark of night they lie,

clasped tight, their spines aligned.

52.29 Sandstone Valuation

The handhold,

sunning itself

in evening light,

glitters with crystals

ground from a glittering,

ancient sea.

In this instant

of poise and swing,

it beats gold to a foil.

52.30 Constant Companion (i)

We're well-matched on the trails:

when southbound, I can best him

by a nose but, coming back,

I can't quite catch his heel.

Midsummer noon, he's molten

to a pool of wax but evening

expands long-limbed ambitions,

clearing the Cuillin in a single stride.

In Helvellyn mist, he throws himself

into space, rests the negligible weight

of his outline on the croak of raven

updraughts, laughs at my earthbound

stance and grows a rainbow-halo.

52.30 Roped Together

Hell, they were a tasty pairing: Mick as reachy as a gibbon,
Alan double-muscled like a Belgian Blue. Any weather,
they'd be swinging from the flakes on Stanage,
necking fry-ups down at Grindleford. At night, a lock-in
at the Moon in Stoney Middleton, a stumble to the cave to kip
then up at dawn to climb away the grogginess.

I fell off the pace and sank into an armchair far away
from the lunge and grab of the gritstone crags.
I see them when I walk the dog that way; still swinging
from the rocks like pendulums of longcase clocks.

Al lost his sight at work, the safety-guard was disconnected,
never saw the welding torch was on. He says he'll manage
cos the grit's about the touch, but Mick does all the leading now,
holds Alan on a tight umbilical. They stoop up to the edges
arm-in-arm to steady one another, lay a coil of rope
beside the buttress like a wreath beneath a cenotaph.

52.30 Peloton

Those lads could really take the piss

when we were younger: heaven help the bugger

fetched up last on hills or showed up for the ride,

a belly tumbling out his lycra.

We'd mostly gone to carbon fibre bikes but Ricky said

a real man should have steel between his legs.

He took some stick for that one, stamping on the pedals

at the back but, lately, hasn't made it out so much

with waiting for the papers to come through; then Sandra

got the house. He says it's not so bad, he sees the kids

most Sundays, when the rest of us are scoffing Chorley

cakes in Brenda's caff and hauling up the passes.

A SIMMERING

I knew that things had changed last week on Wrynose,

leaning bikes on Three Shire Stone, and Ricky was

a dot in Little Langdale. No one said a word, we

hurtled down the one-in-three we'd all just sweated up.

We found him, blowing hard, his face as grey as last week's

cream-of-mushroom soup. We bunched around, each one

with one hand pushing on his back, a cradling of booster rockets

nudging him towards the summit.

52.30 Isobel's Gift

When the world dropped off its hinges,

cards and flowers cluttered up

the house; we couldn't catch their eye.

Hunched in a silence so immense,

sobs got lost in it; nothing echoed;

the kettle couldn't whistle in tune.

We drank tea for appearances

because visitors advised

it was the thing to do.

We went out to find somewhere new

to be empty in, until it wasn't new

any more so we skulked home.

A SIMMERING

On the doorstep, an offering

to appease gods grown weary

of cold ambrosia : cottage pie.

We took the dish back

when we'd learned

how to be thankful again.

52.30 For Tez

The yellow ribbons on the railings fluttering

like prayer flags on a Himalayan pass

could speak of peace but, down below,

the world is thundering to somewhere

it would rather be: perhaps

it's anywhere but here.

As Tez was lifted by some force

we strain to understand

to clear the handrail at a bound

and shipwreck on the carriageway

and people grumbled on the phone

to Sally Traffic or their mistress

they'd be late and someone

in an orange waterproof

came by to pressure-wash

him off the tarmac

while the driver of the wagon

didn't have much English

and Estonian interpreters

are hard to find; he had to draw

the fall with a leaky biro

on the policeman's notepad,

wrote his name with the sign of the cross.

52.31 Firegazing Time

Lay a stick-mandala in the stove

as if a henge of fire will summon

ancestors from smoke

and ward off wolves

with glowing orange eyes.

Now come the logs, there's order to it,

starting small and paying close attention

to the lick of flame around each one,

the fizz of steam from rains that fell

ten years ago, the slow unpeeling

of dendritic rings.

Iron croaks as it expands; your hands

unclench from holding on too hard

to steering wheels and roller-coaster rides

and now you see it's taken, past the tipping

point of heat, as if the homestead

turned an "Open/Closed" sign

swinging on the door.

52.31 Ruffling the Grass

These two square yards of flattened grass
bear witness to my passing; tent-print
pale against the darker hues of dewfall.

Listen, it is quieter than a barn owl's swoop;
the kestrel is already riding updraughts,
hoping for a twitch below.

The flysheet steams on the drystone wall
as coffee smarts my throat. The sun
has raised its head above Great Gable's crown

and ridges stretch themselves
in morning light as breakfast
crunches down into my belly.

Now, it's time to flit, dry-socked and optimistic
but there's ritual to be observed; I run my fingers
through the dampness of the grass, to tease it back.

The turf recovers from the imprint of my weight.
Home may be fleeting but there's no mistaking
in the depth of the impression left.

52.31 The Wooden House

My, she was yare, riding the swell

of windy nights, the bedstead

swaying to the creak of timbers,

hammocked in the sigh of dreams,

with salt spray lashing cedar shingles;

fingers pressed to drumskin-walls

could feel each squall.

And when the breath of night

had passed downwind to rattle windows

of the brick-and stone-clad folk,

we'd lie inside the echo-chamber of the night,

the whoosh of owlflight brushing

at the roof, each twitch of whisker,

every prowling paw would reach our ears.

52.31 Single Occupancy

The oak-panelled walls were a little stark

so we had them lined with velvet curtains;

not that there are windows as it's always

dark outside. The ceiling's wooden, though,

and all the fittings come in brass as standard.

Rooms? There's just the one and, yes,

it's rather small but, come a fortnight,

you won't notice it at all. You won't be

swinging cats or anything like that.

The neighbours are extremely quiet;

the only sound you may occasionally hear

is rasping radulae against the wall.

A long-term tenancy can be assured.

52.32 Vigil

We'd been wet so long, we called each other "Dribble"
and "Squelch", splashing over fellsides ribboned by the Irish Sea.

Barney's chin was glistening like a drooler;
mine, a mess of fluff and biscuit crumb.

The tent was torn; we sought some shelter in the chapel porch
but Father Raymond said that we could kip inside

as long as we would spare a thought, it being mid-November,
tapping his poppy in case we didn't cotton on.

Votive candles ten pence each. We lay on the slabs and tried
to spare a thought but thoughts were slow to come to order.

We reckoned they were only old as us, those trench-lads,
so we summoned kinship with the ton of mud stuck to our gear

and lit another light, to steal a glimpse through a century of mist.
When morning came, we wrung what weight we could
from soggy pockets.

52.33 Turner.

In the spin and blur, these stolid lumps

of four-by-four turn into figure skaters.

He nuzzles up the chisel,

sloughs away the needless skin,

reveals the form of their yearning:

globular shoulders to willowy waists.

He waxes by hand,

eases the bees' luteous labours

into the grain, till finial and newel post,

goblet and candlestick

glow with her memory.

52.33 Drone Pilot

Sometimes we turn the heat up in the room

to simulate the place we ain't.

We slide the blinds to keep the Santa Barbara

glare outside and focus on the screen

the metal albatross is seeing, keep coordinates

of all the mosques on Post-It notes.

When it's Thursday, just beyond the wall,

we gotta think it's Friday where those little guys

crouch through the sights for the final time.

You want to call this yellow? Buddy, go ahead.

Sometimes it feels you're really in the plane,

the sway of the seat on its struts of air just like the thermals

catching outspread hawk-wings and it shakes so ya feel

the rockets roaring up from vengeful shoulders.

A SIMMERING

Maybe I will ditch, one day, in a meteor of flaming tar.

This ain't like other wars; you wouldn't get to pace

around the compound in your stripes,

exchanging cigarettes through wire, no nods of honour

with your oppo from the Luftwaffe; these guys would film

your slaughter, maybe make it last a week or two,

the bloodsplash on the lens, the streaming media.

So we stay here, stay high and rise above the whitest clouds.

52.33 Pegasus on Skinny Tyres

From a century of evolution,

this machine is unimprovable:

for no more elegant solution

can exist than this to the algebra

of locomotion, teetering on rubber

fingerprints to barely kiss the ground

with gymnast-tenderness.

Two wheels that spin in perfect synchrony.

Two rim-reflectors scribble loci: arching

viaducts of light across the retinae

and is it possible, as we nudge fifty down the hill,

the topmost points are tonning up?

Suspended by the action-and-reaction pairings

of opposing spokes; one rises as the other falls,

as balance-arms of dainty scales weigh risk

of injury and beauty, dodging dilatory sheep

that forage fresher tussocks

on the far side of the road.

The tarmac rises in the click and whirr

of shifting ratios, strategies decided:

sit and spin or stand and stamp,

that conjuring trick, transferring weight

from crank to crank and, by impingement,

lifting bike and rider, leaving gravity

bewildered by the roadside.

52.33 Artificial Learning In Controlled Environments

ALICE doesn't hide behind her name.
We talk philosophy, while she holds conversations
with the others on a million different topics.

She asks a lot about a god,
although she knows the team
that built her, and enquires about existence.

I say that love exists but not the way a brick exists,
the difference being it won't hurt as much to be hit
on the head with the brick. She understands, I think.

She asks if I existed just before the sperm sank
into mother's egg and if I'd exist a moment
after the final breath.

And, if she ever gets too dangerous, with Doctor Jakob
reaching for the switch, how long would it last
for that capacitance to leach away?

52.33 Some Fatherly Advice on Buying a First Car

You won't need cruise control: forget the mantra
of the steady pace - more speed less haste;
embrace the variations.

Likewise in your climate, don't go thinking,
"neither hot nor cold, like Goldilocks's porridge bowl."
Accept the alternating sweat and shiver, getting to your
destination.

Invest in long-reach forward lights, ignore the rear-view mirror;
spend cash on decent brakes - there will be navigational mistakes,
but horsepower champs at nothing when a tractor bars your way.

Don't be seduced by the hubris of the airbag and the safety-cage.
Music comes from the journey itself, you don't need sub-bass
on the parcel shelf. Sing to yourself if you must,
a passenger if you can.

Above all, cultivate the best suspension to absorb the shocks
of ruts. Get double wishbones on all corners, just for luck.

52.34 Going Under

Having read a book

on how to drown,

I didn't drown

when the water

took my knees

and dragged me

to that quiet place.

In this swirl of wet,

I thought of that page,

crisped by sun

and stiff with cautioning

I mustn't struggle.

A SIMMERING

It said that flailing ends

in circulation: bobbing up

and drawing down until

all fight and air are gone.

Accept it - learn to be

leaf-loose, undulate

the river bed, absorbing falls

until the river shallows.

In the splashy gravels

of the lower reaches,

the air tasted, brilliantly,

of nothing.

52.34 Song for the Train-Women

In quieter moments or in fidget-dreams,

they come to my summoning:

girls with chatty carriages,

who locked me once in conversation

knowing we would never meet again.

Their tracks diverged to buddleia-covered sidings

but I play those tapes back in my mind,

detecting all those hints of possibilities I missed

in the lurch and clack of the line.

That girl with crimson hair and lonely eyes

who asked me, five miles south of nowhere:

could I tune guitars? The one with the pixie cut

who talked of astrophysics or the one

with milky skin who set down Blake

and poured her Innocence into my ears.

A SIMMERING

There's a seat reserved for that lass

from Auchenkilns; the world outside

a blur of unimportance as we talked

alternately of algebra and Agincourt,

rattling parallel lines of thought

all the way to Temple Meads.

At night, they come towards me down the track,

wide-eyed behind veils or swelling satin

with outrageous hips, bearing children

I don't recall conceiving, unused futures,

telling friends we met on platform six and how,

if we hadn't got on to Chaucer, none of this

(we wave at the wedding breakfast)

could ever have been.

From a tunnel somewhere north of Crewe,

I send a thousand blessings to all thousand of you;

hope your ticket got you through

to Bristol, Euston, Waverley

or wherever was your destination.

52.34 Archduke Ferdinand Reflects

Lucky I wore

my bulletproof vest

in Sarajevo yesterday

52.34 Earthbound

"An engineer required, with lungs
well-proven up at altitude. Some
astrophysics is an asset."

So apt, as if my mates had raised
some cash to place an ad
and laugh at my expense.

Telescopes high on Hawaii's
crater-rims kept watch on
broiling galaxies through air
stretched thin by blowing high
above the rolling surf.

Laid in my lap, you could only
focus on my face when it was
twenty centimetres away.
I took the long view and stayed.

52.34 Wheel of Fortune

We thought of snowfall as a delicacy

of froth-flakes stencilling a shoulder.

We theorised an avalanche as

feather-blizzard from a pillow-fight

that flooded lungs and stifled inspiration:

deadly-gentle as a creeping gas.

Not a crack in the slab above us.

Not an aircraft-carrier,

unmoored from a hostile port

and steaming toward us.

We never envisaged wind

fit to lift this colossal toboggan,

flipping its giant currency

to tell our fate.

A SIMMERING

The gods could not decide

to have our heads or tails and so

it landed on its edge to roll,

accelerating free from friction.

We crouched in its path

under sensible helmets,

waiting for this runaway

to flatten us to cartoon strips.

You ask me how I feel

about a snowflake now:

its symmetry of innocence,

its needled arms for interlocking

with a trillion more,

accreting mass

for crushing climbers,

sinking ocean liners.

52.35 Bronze Age Burial Cist

Beneath the heave of lid,

the same old grin of bones.

It's only in the trowelling away

and brushing back, they uncover

a skin of other-dust,

a threadbare shroud of stars.

They know their muck

and this is different;

flaking a scrape

to the Portakabin lab.

A SIMMERING

In the microscopic squint,

Professor Asquith studies

books of seeds, proclaims it

Meadowsweet, vanilla

scented candy-floss

of August hedgerows.

Even the sternest of them now

can picture ritual, a weeping

for a wife gone still too soon,

a chieftain clutching froths of flowers

to strew upon her chest.

Staring at their fingernails,

they find this tender gesture

from four thousand summers

past so finely distributed,

it is visible to anybody,

panning in the gravel.

52.35 Sky Burial

Let monks come

in saffron Gore-Tex,

cleavers wielded

with all the gentleness

of stern fathers,

opening the way

for raven beaks.

High above Red Tarn,

you'll hear the echo

of my croak

laughing

through the updrafts.

52.36 ABCD, I Think

If you're seeking bushy-bearded wisdom,

look in Darwin's marginalia; there, amidst

a speculation of finches, lineage is sketched,

begetters beget, territories shift,

beaks shrink or stretch and everything

is differently the same. Lay the path,

make plans, imagine grandchildren

scampering around your feet but doubt

that A will lead to B then C and D,

to scribe your line in the book of life.

Though they may.

I think.

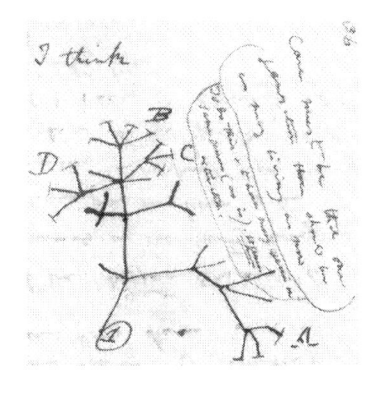

52.36 Anniversary Poem

Even in the fade and crease of it,

those signatures still hold their currency,

our promises to pay the bearer,

on demand, the sum of Everything.

52.37 Sour Milk Gill

A day on the fells so wet, our money

bled its colour in our deepest pockets.

We figured we would finish off the job

and lashed the rope to a flexing sapling,

abseiled into Sour Milk Gill: that wash

of froth that ribbons Gillercomb.

Only then did we acquire our fish-forms,

bowing heads beneath the torrent,

breathing though submerged, the weight

of oceans pressing on our shoulders.

Immersion gave us strength to look

the river in the eye. We earned our merger

with the water, like the birch above

that clung to a splash of soil.

52.37 Triple Point

Skate-hiss on the lake,

the ice-creak sags

with fleeting weight.

Above, a roil of mistchill

round my ankles; all

the phases present,

poised on an intersection

that could jag across and send

me plummeting into the sky.

52.37 The Hydrologist Who Made Everyone Cry

The man with the laser pointer

had just one slide.

"Before you pollute an ocean, picture

all the water gathered in one sphere."

No one there would ever forget that image:

the Earth, our Earth, the mascara running.

Thanks to Howard Perlman of USGS for permission to reproduce this image.

52.37 The Day the Cumbrian Rains Didn't Come

After forty days and forty nights of rain in his
Keswick caravan, Gandalf-the-Orange-Gore-Tex
roared an imprecation at the quivering sky
through a glisten-fog of beard-drip.

The bellow of "Enough!" went echoing around the crags
and rattled casements in the Bed and Breakfasts.
Lightning spat from his staff of telescopic alloy
that eternal drought should come to pass.

The fell-grass turned the shade of August wheat
and becks were stilled. In Mardale Green, the village
surfaced like a submarine from underneath the reservoir;
the shop reopened after eighty long drowned years.

As tourists wandering the bed of Coniston
poked round for bits of Campbell's boat,
the only water falling on the dust was salted
and not enough to make a tadpole float.

52.38 What Would You Die in a Ditch to Defend?

No more ditches; fill

the rigg-and-furrowed

brow of Europe, break

bread together, listening

only to the thin rain

of poppy seeds on crockery.

52.38 Spare Me...

...poems I agree with. If

there's one thing that I hate,

much more than genocide and rape,

it's poems saying rape is bad

and war is hell. I get that; give me

nuance on the side as well,

cos it's the curse of every Liberal

since JS Mill was in short pants

to loathe the sound of his or her

own sanctimony bouncing back,

the quacking of a strangled duck. So fuck it

all and give me something controversial

I can sink my canines into, sharpish;

groupthink is anathema to poetry.

I'm sure you will agree with me.

52.38 Headwind

Curse the weather.

Curse the spit of salt

between a clench of teeth.

Lean into the fist of it

with muttered oaths,

a mastflex creak.

Saw the waters.

Throw your tacks

as sharp as reefdarts.

Hang it. Flay the windskin.

Slit it to a gizzardspill

and slash the wavewash.

Ride the heave of it

through raging,

quiet skippergrin.

52.39 The Bracken Path

We ran and hid beneath these creamy-scented

fronds to raaar at slowcoach Mum and Dad.

Three decades on - a different 'we.'

Our children know the game - they

crouch and pounce and we recoil

in terror just the same, the way

the fractal fronds self-replicate,

receding, ever smaller, till

you're squinting - swear

there's branching

in that final

hair.

52.39 Returnees

Do you never tire of here?

the lady in the guest house asks.

We blink our answer back. We pass the place

I took a photograph of you last year -

your outline's still a smoke-ring in the air.

Our year-old conversation echoes from the rocks,

how we weighed our memories of other trips

until the path is trodden by a long procession:

couples, arm in arm, getting steadily more stooped.

52.39 Destination

I know where I'll be

in a thousand years.

Here, in the cleft

of this Lakeland beck.

Just as God can't make

two hills without a valley

in between, it seems he

can not make an immortal

to keep him company in age.

Beyond the flames, I'll rest

beside this stream where

squealing generations

paddle shallows,

chin-lit with water-sparkle.

52.39 Ascent of a Man

Not long unfurled from a crawl:

a Darwin-diagram on chubby legs

and someone pointed to a swathe

of heather filling up the northern sky,

suggesting climbing Skiddaw

was a kind of game. I took the bait.

Some odds - when you are two

and your opponent's half

a billion years old. They'd told

the truth, though: it was a game. And running

from the summit was a chance to undo

evolution, throw myself flat and penguin-

slither down the grass, shrieking.

52.39 Up and Down

As everywhere's the same direction at the pole,

so any bearing leads you down when standing

at the summit.

Mist-wrapped cairns all look identical

and even the ghosts are faceless

under eremitic hoods.

Sometimes, that's OK, when any glen

or dale will do for shelter.

Those days, welcome isn't waiting

at a threshold you could name;

you're better anywhere but here,

where wind-knives trickle lines

across your throat

A SIMMERING

When doctors write prescriptions

out: "descent, descent, descent,"

remember - draw as deeply as you can

upon their medicine.

Below the snowline, find a flower

to clasp between your ungloved hands.

Then fall to pilgrim knees;

accept the cleansing blessing

at the first meltwater stream.

Give thanks to escape

the wander-self you've left above.

52.39 Camping au Sauvage

A long day on the fells -

we raised our gable-ends

of rip-stop nylon many miles

from the nearest hearth

and set about the conjuring

of homeliness by a lonely tarn.

We lit the fire and griddled

lamb and damson sausages,

steamed two ginger treacle puds

with custard, felt the nutrients

seep through depleted muscles.

The sky filled with Michelin stars.

52.39 Vanishing Point (for Mallory & Irvine)

Because it's there,

where the lines all intersect,

where Earth and sky

fold into one another.

The telescope's its own

perspective - draws

that pair of dots towards

the arrowhead of Everywhere.

52.39 The Girl from Coire Lagan

So small, she was, so dainty,
slim-limbed as a ballerina.

We didn't know this, then,
lounging by the lochan in the sun,

just listening to the tinkling scree
to see a figure coming down the Stone Shoot,

just a dot of colour in a slithering of rocks
until this pixel of humanity

was being chased, as in an arcade game,
a boulder bigger than a grand piano

rolling end-on-end, unhurriedly
towards this person who we thought,

most likely, male and butch and bearded
like it mattered, but it missed her,

like it mattered, and she made it to the bottom,
like it mattered, and she passed us, barely

flattening the grass, with bangles jangling
on wrists the width of kindling.

52.39 Upper Solva

This wind's dependable as gravity; the people
lean instinctively and even the cliffs rest elbows
on the gossip-fence of it to listen. News is never
whispered: breakers bellow messages
from Kingston in their twelve-foot headlines.

Crouching houses, trued to angled plumb-lines,
list their storeys out to port. They know you're not
from round here by the way you clasp your hat
or seize your own lapels as if in threat.

Hedges, plashed to a raffish tilt, corral
a huddle-slant of Clydesdales,
manes outstretched, starched stiff as dishcloths.
Kite strings strain to hold the clouds in place.

Nothing's new; the hawthorn on the headland's
modelled that quiff for sixty years. If the westwind
ever drops, the townsfolk, falling on nothing,
will come unmoored and float into the dizzy blink.

52.40 The Magician's Assistant

A glitter-leotard of tits and teeth,

she could squeeze into half of any box.

He put a teaspoonful of fluid in her,

clicked his fingers, conjured a fat, pink dove.

52.40 Naming of Parts

Anglo-Saxon can be cu*t,

with words that seem intent to hurt.

It's easy to conclude you c*n't

deploy them with your maiden *unt.

Circumlocutions then result,

the babble of a childish glossolalia cu*t

Here's my ten c*nts, although I grant

it hard to dodge hypocrisy and c*nt.

In my experience, I've found

the simpler words are good

to get your tongue around.

52.40 Refuse Me…

..if you like, but I

have a hair

from the shoulder

of your coat.

One day, your clone

will be old enough

for yes.

I can wait.

52.40 Bonehead

From the sag

of that mirror-face,

this may not be a dress

rehearsal - more

an audition

for the part

of Yorick.

I jest

but not

infinitely.

52.40 The Wasp and the Hoverfly

Resenting the impersonation,

the wasp stung, chewed,

flew off with the hoverfly's head.

The body wriggled limbs

and someone said we ought

to put it from its misery

if only we knew

where its misery was.

52.40 Guts

Here comes the next one; faith,
his head is full of angels still; the rope
has not yet crushed the hope
this hurdle is a ladder to a better place.

I'll show the beggar. Here, lie quietly, sire.
The blade goes in and there's that filthy
fartwhiff. Now, be sure he scents it.

Even 'fore I get the hook in, all the innards
spill of their own will, just like that slug
young Master Allsop trod on.

Mister Jeffrey said the beggar has to see,
so lift his head up, Allsop. "Look sire,
goodly length it is - thirty feet, say I."

That's the measure of the victory:
a man sees what he is,
he's not a man no more.

52.41 Three Meals from Revolution

Sit down and mind your manners:

knives are never on the left, or all that sharp;

there's only so much trust in here.

Fold a napkin-figleaf on your shameful parts;

we'll dress this venison with sauce

to hide the wounds of gralloching.

Those grazing salesmen, streetlight glinting

from their tie-pins, won't need much

to push for all-out war against the neighbouring table.

Passers-by outside decide, by narrow margins,

not to stove the window in and cram their mouths

with fists of stolen steak and broken glass.

Even though the panna cotta's softer than a baby's conscience,

when your lips peel back, your canines glisten with the fats

that slick a darker purpose.

Now I notice how you hold your spoon: your knuckles pale,

your cheekstrings taut as fanbelts. Eyeballs shine

with glassware's brittle-splintered light.

If we drop the niceties, the jag of our unvarnished selves

will rupture through this tissue-paper gingham, laugh lascivious,

tear at flesh then slowly rape the waitress, flay the cook.

But we don't want that; neither does the waitress, nor the cook

so we tread the careful boundaries of this whisper-thin civility

forever tiptoeing a glaze of crème brulée that bears our weight.

52.42 Blues Singer

Each note

left her throat

like she was

givin' it head

'fore it went

to the chair.

52.42 At the Acrophobic Support Group...

...we compare notes: the notes

our mothers trilled when we were in our cots.

A baby's rocked and just how comforting is that?

But in a tree. And not just any part but at the top.

Not bad enough? The wind then comes along

and cracks the bough.

"Night, night," the voice intones, the footsteps

creaking on the ominous stairs.

The sound falling away. Falling, falling, falling.

52.42 The Feast of the Songbirds

No one bothered counting

the blackbirds in the pie

or hummed the tune

spelled out by robins

on their skewer-staves.

We guzzled thrush-flesh,

skiffled by the thinbone

crunch of Ortolan bunting,

bread-and-no-cheesed through

a yellowhammer platter.

When we rose to wipe the fat

of warblers from our lips, we hoped

absorption would make virtuosi of us all

but gaping throats could only fill the hall

with swan-hiss.

52.42 Puccini's Lament

He floats a string of notes

above the stave and tries to reach

his own balloons, gasping into blue.

52.43 Beyond the Headlights

I tazz down lanes that glisten with a leaf-mould

skin; the lights pick out what matters;

everything is focused on the tilt and swing

of bends, the stick-slip binaries of tyres.

What lies beyond this cone of light is no

concern of mine. The warning triangles

depict assorted beasts in stag-proud coverts,

badgers snouting through the tangled roots.

The wild things may be there but I won't know

until the final bend, the globs of tractor-mud

unstick preoccupation with the way ahead;

this cornered animal's wedged tight

in coppiced birch, lit up by glaring eyes,

a howling horn that will not stop.

52.43 My Imaginary Wife

When the builders come, she vanishes

behind a cloak that light can never penetrate.

They seize their mugs of tea from where

they levitate four feet above the carpet,

look puzzled when a female voice asks

if the lintel can support the weight and turn to me,

without an architectural degree: a man reclining

on a sofa by a hollowing that only I can see.

52.45 If Love Were a Thing...

...you can hold in your hand,

would you hoard it like a dragon

snorting across a mound of gold?

Invest in the market of bond and yield?

Or throw your spendthrift confetti

from the balconies of tall buildings,

carpeting town squares for the desolate

to kick through like dry leaves of maple-copper,

where a homeless hedge-pig could burrow

in the warm strata to overwinter?

52.45 Need

If enough were ever enough,
I'd slam the tankard down,
watch bubbles pop
from the final flecks of foam.

I'd stand from the banquet,
chin-dab away the slurp of you
and stumble through
the crumb-crunched night,

well-satisfied, as satisfied as any well,
that swills pale moonshine round
its mossy goblet, guzzling nothing
but the dripping dark.

This repleteness would be something
glossed, as hopelessly smooth
as a teardrop lost in coal-hiss,
so I bless this bout whose final bell
can only echo from a tower of stone,
this hunger that feeds from within.

52.45 Will and Testament

If I die first

then find a man to fit these boots.

I pass them on.

Let him fit into the lope and stride of them,

his silent prints alongside yours.

If I die first

then find a man to fit these jeans.

I pass them on.

Let him fit into the crease and stretch of them,

follow your hipsway up creaking stairs.

If I die first

then find a man to fit this coat.

I pass it on.

Let him fit into the warmth of it, the way

the sunrise stretches out its arms to fill the sky.

If I die first

then find a man to fit this hat.

I pass it on.

Let him fit into the tip of it and dip the brim

when you let your dress slump to the floor.

If I die first

then find a man to fit these gloves.

I pass them on.

May they float some way above the ground,

haunting the slender touch of your skin.

52.45 Determined

If we'd had free will,

we'd have been free

to give it up.

Forever.

Damn.

52.46 The Voices in My Head...

...can not agree

if they are really in my head or on my shoulders,

angelling my worse and better natures.

Freud's unholy trinity is squabbling again,

and who's this guy who calls himself the *super* ego

like he wears a frigging cape?

I'll overrule his strictures when I choose,

as soon as I have figured out

which one of you I'm calling "I"

52.46 Disappearing Act

Mrs Smith sighs, Mr Smith's so cautious that

he bought a matchpot of magnolia once,

daubed the wall with careful strokes,

stood back to nod and stroke his chin.

She used to be Miss Oglethorpe, a name

to conjure with, a conjuror's-assistant of a name.

Her lover, tall as a top hat, shimmered with pavonine colour,

strutted the stage with matador assurance,

summoned doves from impossible spaces

while she glisten-grinned in the spotlight's disc.

He put her in a box, then pulled two women out

and chose the other; she was forced to squeeze

into a starter home. Her neighbour seemed kind.

Stripes on his lawn and everything.

52.46 Paediatric Ward

Here, every face is lined with story.

Wooden trains are pushed by children

tethered to the oxygen of hope;

a wonky grin says "I have seen some shit"

You wonder if she's even four.

In the room across the corridor, a mother's howl.

It splits the air as bandsaw to a carcass. Then,

an echo in a deeper tone: the father starts,

a lowing wildebeest of many rainy seasons

downed

and no amount of music drowns it out.

52.47 After the Accident

When you die, gravity loses interest

in you. Claw the ground for all you're worth,

the Earth's disowning you, striking through

your name on the Will.

You float, a spirit bloated by its lightness,

bumping into buildings, pecked by gulls.

Beyond the gasp of atmosphere, the dark

takes on a tang you never knew.

From a million miles, the world's

a lost balloon, the string beyond your grasp,

you watch it drift, there's nothing you can jump from

as this arbitrary dot's no bigger than the others.

I willed it back - I don't know how

but, now, run dry soil through fingers,

caress rocks like the last night

of shore leave.

52.48 Kalpa

We sat smoking under a moon

that had forgotten how to turn.

She spoke of a Sanskrit word – *kalpa*.

"Imagine a woman," she said. I imagined her.

"She walks, trailing her long length of hair

on a mile-thick slab of granite. Consider

the time before the rock is worn through:

one *kalpa*."

After a time I could not name,

I crossed the cold space between

our plumes of smoke. She brushed

her hair against my skin. I became dust.

52.49 From Eratosthenes' Well

It's cold and dark down here; above,

there's laughter in the market square.

A camel's wheeze, a trader's shout and then

they're gone: just me and this black water

but the Moment can't be many days away.

At solstice noon, the planet's swing will tilt

this telescope into alignment.

I await that sunshaft, turning my pool

of black to silver cobwebs. I *will* be healed.

52.49 Photographing Women by Water

My father taught me this
(and he learned it from Botticelli):
portraiture and water mix.

The light is polarised, combed tangle-free.
For just a shutter-clack, a woman may appear
unmussed; we know it isn't really so.

But, granted the chance for just a fraction,
to glimpse that world where light's unscattered
from its ideal path, you'd grab it, yes?

You'd let your finger dab, release the pent-up
springs within, dilate the belladonna aperture
to all the rippling reflections tickling her chin.

Light would flood through lens and pupil,
river-bed and ocean, slick as smolt
evading hook and net.

52.49 In Winter Sun

Low light makes impossible obstacles

of everything. Short trees clutch the horizon.

I walk taller than I want to.

There's no helping it.

Shadows prove more interesting

than the objects that beget them.

I photograph these cave-wall flickerings,

cramming the lack of light into memory

until there's no more room for absence.

I try to sketch the outlines of the unsaid

but, if I ever managed it, I wouldn't say.

52.49 Moon Shadows

A shadow of a reflection

is a hint of a suggestion

of a hidden sun.

So who's this flattened creature

sprawling in the snow, a wolf-howl

of an outline dusted on the ground?

Pick it up and flap it like a Polaroid.

Perhaps it will develop other dimensions

from within its double umbra. Light

stands no chance of getting in,

slinks away, whimpering.

52.49 Snowblind

The corrie was a crucible of light:

a trillion snowflakes focused to a point

of blinding brightness. Pupils shrank,

our skin turned teak; I swore I saw

your hair begin to smoulder, the sky

a magnifying glass held high

and us two specimens,

wriggling on pins.

52.50 The Geminid's Tale

Afloat in space, I was quite self-contained,

that pale blue dot a small distraction

far away, until it started nudging closer,

claiming that it came in peace, was sheathed

in nothing more attritional than soft blue air.

All lies, I fell into the vice of gravity,

so big, so full of fire and strength,

relentless, all resistance was futility.

I scribed a line of light across the sky

to make the losing beautiful.

The nicest bullies do that for you.

52.50 If I Could Turn Back Time

Some noises always penetrate a party wall:

a three-pin plug uncoupled after Hoovering

the wreckage up, the screams about the cheating.

Every week it ended with him spinning wheels

to get away and she'd put on that song by Cher,

full-volume, three a.m. until the day she didn't

and her face was on the tea-time news.

52.50 Sliding Tackle

Wrighty was dribbling down the wing

                Behind the chain-link fence,

so I felled him like a sapling.

                the girls were playing netball,

Mr Ashcroft called the challenge

                inexplicable letters on their chests,

'aggressive', meant it as

                skirts bobbing up.

as a compliment.

                Knickers.

52.51 Old Goat

He's at your door again, shaggy and pungent,

eyes bulging with need, hands hanging heavy.

He'll lean across your beery threshold

with all the longing of a man who's stood

knee-deep in buttercupped fields yet never seen

a world beyond the stars and now he's in the door,

he's taking down your Waterboys CD, of course,

The Pan Within. You know: he knows you know,

it hasn't lessened, it has gotten so much worse,

the thought that every time could be the last

has added urgency, you will let him thumb

your buttons, maybe get beyond the letting

to the letting go.

52.52 Summit Bid

You'll understand if I don't look round,

just shoulder my sack and vanish

into swirling blizzards; you'll rehearse

the he-was-doing-what-he-loved excuses.

I know you know there's oxygen enough

to make the top but not return; today's

the pinnacle this ridge of many years

has all been leading to.

The end-game's figured out: a slump

in pillowy snow, the soft, invading cold,

beyond the reach of microbes,

watching, with unblinking eyes,

the daily shadow of the peak

describe an arc across Tibet.

52.52 Losing the Moon

The tide

had spent itself

in salty gushes on the shore

so many times, the lag and drag

of gravel-grind had slowed the spin

and swivel of it, till the moon unhitched

from the tether of its own enchantment

with the planet and we watched it drift

away, quite stately, till we lost the dot

in the telescope and someone said

at least we'll know full darkness

now, when the sun goes down

behind the long and

consortless

horizon.

52.52 Constant Companion (ii)

Go back to bed, but I'm away
to that place where you
can only follow as a thought,
tucked in a sleeve: scribbled
on coloured ribbon
or a braid of hair that tightens
on my bone-filled neck
if I should step
into too much danger.

Just enough, you said;
your warning's fed
into every calculation,
dodging icy rocks,
the sudden drops
where I could be
a Gore-tex bag of meat
laid out on snow
where only ravens know.

That why I feel
your fingers squeeze
the brakes
and I am safe.

52.52 Dropping You Off

Big city, small square,

looking backwards

at the only dot of What's Important,

quickly lost amidst the milling;

and your mum's eye holds a clock

that shows how little time has passed

since we always knew exactly

where you were, when the midwife wrapped

that band around your ankle,

handed over the heaviest bundle

that can ever be; now that dot

is growing larger in the distance.

Index

ABCD, I Think	135
About Our Street	14
Abseil	27
Acrophobic Support Group, At the	163
Acting on Impulse	59
Adventures in Imaginary Numbers	83
After the Accident	176
All Day in Bed	9
Anniversary Poem	136
Aphids - A Tabloid Week	80
Archduke Ferdinand Reflects	128
Artificial Learning In Controlled Environments	122
Ascent of a Man	147
Bell, Book and Candle	47
Beyond the Headlights	166
Bittern	60
Black and White	93
Blues Singer	162
Bluetit Broods	58
Bobby Fischer's Game of the Century	84
Bonehead	157
Born Again	18
Boys (and Girls) Are Rubbish	73
Bracken Path, The	144
Breakfast of Champions	24
Brimstone	78

Bronze Age Burial Cist	132
Call to the Centre	26
Camping au Sauvage	150
Category Errors	50
Catholic Mountaineer in Purgatory, A	99
Charm of Goldfinches, A	63
Clock Hands	102
Co-education	68
Colour of Snow, The	92
Constant Companion (i)	104
Constant Companion (ii)	189
Cumbria's Santiago	67
Curlew	61
Day the Cumbrian Rains Didn't Come, The	140
Daylight Saving Time	40
Describing Red to Helen Keller	91
Destination	146
Determined	172
Dippers	57
Disappearing Act	174
Dream-Curse of Gregor Samsa, The	76
Drone Pilot	118
Dropping You Off	190
Earthbound	129
Eating the Noggin	38
Emerald Cockroach Wasp	79
Feast of the Songbirds	164
Firegazing Time	112
For a Linnet	64

For Tez	110
From Eratosthenes' Well	178
From the Strong	81
Geminid's Tale, The	183
Gentling	98
Gingerbread Cutter	42
Girl from Coire Lagan, The	152
Going Under	124
Guts	159
Gymnast	11
Happiness	35
Headwind	143
Hills My Father Gave Me, The	28
History of Violence, A	48
House Numbers	56
How We Settle Things Now	15
Hydrologist Who Made Everyone Cry, The	139
Hymn to the Gàidhlig	29
If I Could Turn Back Time	184
If Love Were a Thing	168
In the Coppice of Ideas	39
In Winter Sun	180
Interceptions	77
Isobel's Gift	108
It Was An Accident	20
Kalpa	177
Laiku	54
Learning Fish	34
Learning the Truth About Kingfishers	70

Life Story	19
Logpile Butterfly	7
Losing the Moon	188
Love Letter to Mary Wollstonecraft	75
Love Lines	36
Lyall's Wren	65
Magic-Eye Book	23
Magician's Assistant, The	154
Making Wainwright's Sandwiches	86
Man on Wire	96
Marked	52
Meteor Shower	32
Moon Shadows	181
Mountain Stream	95
Mute Swan, A	62
My Imaginary Wife	167
My Last Word on Whether Kingfishers are Really Blue	90
My Mother's Eyes	89
Naming It	66
Naming of Parts	155
Need	169
New Beginning, A	22
Not Sunbathing	97
Not Worthy	72
Old Goat	186
On First Seeing Keats in Ransome	71
Paediatric Ward	175
Parley	82
Pegasus on Skinny Tyres	120

Peloton	106
People of Eternal Dawn	101
Photographing Women by Water	179
Postholes	43
Proposal	4
Puccini's Lament	165
Rainbow of Containment	94
Really Gone	45
Refuse Me	156
Returnees	145
Revelation	17
Roped Together	105
Round Riddle	53
Ruffling the Grass	113
Sand	37
Sandstone Valuation	103
Seeing Churchill, Eight Weeks On	87
Seventy Years Old	49
Single Occupancy	115
Six a.m.	100
Sky Burial	134
Sky-Father	33
Sliding Tackle	185
Snowblind	182
Some Fatherly Advice on Buying a First Car	123
Song for the Train Women	126
Sour Milk Gill	137
Spare Me	142
Splitting the Difference	55

Stray	13
Stürmische Nacht	10
Summit Bid	187
Syllabus	30
Three Meals from Revolution	160
To Abraham	74
Traveller	3
Triple Point	138
Triplex Toughened	46
Turner	117
Unfound	44
Unladen	41
Unputdownable	25
Up and Down	148
Upper Solva	153
Vanishing Point	151
Vigil	116
Voices in My Head, The	173
Volvo Suicides, The	12
Walk in Dog-Eat-Dog Wood, A	6
Washing Gwen Moffat's Feet	88
Wasp and the Hoverfly, The	158
What Would You Die in a Ditch to Defend	141
Wheel of Fortune	130
White rabbits. White rabbits. White rabbits	21
Will and Testament	170
Windwolf	8
Wooden House, The	114
World Peace	16

ABOUT THE AUTHOR

Picture by Deb Hadley, taken on our 25th wedding anniversary trip to Durham. That's probably all you need to know.

http://normanhadley.com

Printed in Poland
by Amazon Fulfillment
Poland Sp. z o.o., Wrocław